CONNECT *to the* UNIVERSE WITHIN

A JOURNEY TO EXPERIENCE
THE HIGHER SELF

SMRUTIPRAVA DASH

BlueRose ONE
Stories Matter
New Delhi • London

BLUEROSE PUBLISHERS
India | U.K.

BlueRose ONE
Stories Matter
NewDelhi • London

For permissions requests or inquiries regarding this publication, please contact:

BLUEROSE PUBLISHERS
www.BlueRoseONE.com
info@bluerosepublishers.com
+91 8882 898 898
+4407342408967

ISBN: 978-93-6261-077-5

Cover Design: Sadhna Kumari
Typesetting: Pooja Sharma

First Edition: June 2024

DEDICATION

For those who ponder question and see,

this book is dedicated to thee.

ACKNOWLEDGEMENT

This book is a culmination of love, understanding, and wisdom.

I extend my sincerest gratitude to every individual who has graced my life with their presence, inspiring and enlightening me along the way. Additionally, I want to express my heartfelt appreciation to the following individuals for their continuous support and contributions to both my journey and the creation of this book.

To my family, unwavering support, understanding, and encouragement throughout this journey.

To my friend, your belief in me never wavered, and your love was my steady anchor through the storms of doubt. your encouragement was the gentle breeze that pushed me forward when I felt stuck in the doldrums of uncertainty.

To my inspiration, your wisdom and guidance were the compass that kept me on course when the path seemed obscured.

To the team at Bluerose Publications, your dedication and hard work turned the sparks of imagination into the flames of reality.

And to you, dear reader, whose presence breathes life into these words, infusing them with purpose and meaning beyond measure. Thank you for giving these words a home in your heart.

With gratitude,

Dash

Smrutiprava Dash

PREFACE

In this profound exploration of the human longing for a blissful universe, we embark on a journey that transcends the boundaries of language, culture, and religion. From the banks of the mightiest river to the presence of abundant food, we find ourselves hungry and thirsty, immersed in a world that holds the promise of fulfilment, yet eludes our grasp. It is within the realm of religion that we seek answers to unveil the secrets of this elusive bliss, for it is a universal yearning that resides within every human heart.

Throughout the ages, the quest for this blissful universe has been the driving force behind the endeavours of nations and the cornerstone of religious teachings. Though expressed in different languages and through diverse faiths, the underlying essence remains the same. Each tradition, in its unique way, strives to convey the truth that is being sought, transcending mere linguistic distinctions.

It is easy to speak of perceiving God in all things, to revel in the idea of finding divinity everywhere. However, the true test arises when we are confronted with the harsh realities of the world. During our daily interactions, when faced with adversity and unexpected challenges, our lofty ideals often falter. The hurt we receive from life can shatter our perceptions, leaving us disillusioned and questioning the very existence of divinity. It is in these moments that we may find ourselves seeing the devil instead of encountering God.

Yet, despite the inherent difficulties, the teachings that prompt us to see God in all things hold profound significance. The purpose lies in perseverance, for true realization cannot be achieved in a single day. The process begins with hearing, then contemplating, and ultimately meditating upon the teachings. Just as the sky is visible to even the lowest of creatures, though seemingly distant, our ideal remains within reach. We must strive to internalize it, allowing it to permeate our being until it resonates in every fibre of our existence.

Thought, the propelling force within us, shapes our perception of the world. By filling our minds with the highest thoughts, by immersing ourselves in their contemplation day after day, month after month, we can gradually transform our consciousness. Failures and setbacks are inevitable, but they are an intrinsic part of life's journey. Without struggles, without the poetry of adversity, life would lose its meaning. Therefore, we must embrace failures as stepping stones, holding fast to our ideals even in the face of repeated disappointments.

The ideal of humanity lies in perceiving divinity in everything and everyone. Should this prove challenging, we can begin by seeing God in one thing, in that which resonates most deeply with our hearts. From there, we can expand our vision, recognizing the divine in every aspect of existence. Infinite life awaits the soul that embarks upon this path, and with patience and perseverance, the ultimate goal can be attained.

The ancient philosophy expounds the concept of Oneness, revealing that all our misery stems from ignorance. The apparent divisions between individuals, nations, and celestial bodies are but illusions. At the core of existence, Unity prevails. By delving beneath the surface, we discover the interconnectedness of all things and beings. The realization of this Oneness dispels delusion and eradicates suffering. In the realm of Reality, there is no death, no sorrow, and no discontent. Perfect Union and Perfect Bliss await those who transcend the limitations of this ignorant world and are connected to the universe within.

As we delve into the depths of these profound teachings, may we be inspired to seek the truth that lies beyond language and cultural barriers. May this exploration awaken within us the recognition of our shared humanity and the unity that underlies the diversity of our experiences. Together, let us embark on this transformative journey, guided by ancient wisdom, in our quest to discover the eternal truths that reside within us all.

Smrutiprava Dash

I'm not expecting blind belief from you.

A person who demands blind belief lowers himself, and if you comply, you lower yourself too. The wise only share their findings after introspection, and they encourage us to do the same. Only then should we believe, not before.

I respect other's viewpoint, and it has its merits. Yet, please don't dismiss mine. Both science and spirituality have practical value. Humanity is moving towards unity. Eventually, everyone will be equally practical in both realms, leading to harmony and unity. We're all striving towards the same goal, overcoming differences through love and cooperation, like a stream flowing towards the ocean of life and bliss.

I don't mind different beliefs, but I oppose teachings that make us weak. I ask everyone: Are we strong? Strength comes from truth. Weakness leads to superstitions and illusions. It makes our minds sick and unable to grasp truth. Strength is essential, it's the cure for the world's problems. The poor, the ignorant, the sinners; all need strength to overcome oppression and ignorance.

CONTENTS

ILLUSION

"Illusion is reminiscent of magic, captivating our senses and blurring the lines between reality and perception."

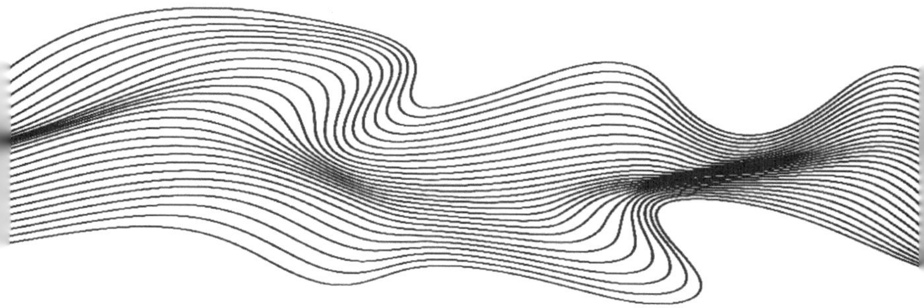

The word illusion originally meant something like magic, and we see this meaning in various other quotes as well. Over time, however, the word illusion disappeared from use, but the idea behind it continued to develop.

“What prevents us from uncovering the mysteries of the universe?” The answer is important: "Because we talk without understanding, we focus on material things, and we chase after desires. So, it's like we're covering up the truth with a mist." Here, the word illusion isn't used, but we understand that our ignorance is like a fog that blocks us from seeing the truth.

Our minds are limited, unable to go beyond certain boundaries like time, space, and causation. Just as we can't jump out of ourselves, we can't go beyond these limits set by the laws of time and space. Trying to understand these laws is pointless because we have to assume their existence to even attempt it.

When we say "this world has no existence," it means it doesn't have absolute existence. It only exists in relation to our minds and the minds of others. We perceive the world through our five senses, but if we had another sense, we might perceive it differently. And if we had yet another sense, it would appear even more different. So, the world doesn't have a real existence because it's not unchangeable, immovable, or infinite. But we can't call it non-existence either because it does exist, and we have to live and work in it. It's like a mix of existence and non-existence.

In our everyday lives, we experience a mix of existence and non-existence. We often feel like we can know everything, but then we hit a wall we can't pass. Our problems call for solutions, but we're limited by our intellect. We're torn between selfish desires and the belief that unselfishness is good. As children, we're optimistic, dreaming big. In youth, we're even more optimistic, struggling to accept things like death and failure. But as we age, life's challenges wear us down, turning us into pessimists. We're constantly pushed around by nature, unsure of where we're headed.

People who have enough to eat and drink often avoid talking about misery because it scares them. They opt to concentrate on the positive aspects of their lives. But others are suffering, and telling them that everything is good won't help. How can they want others to be happy when they are miserable themselves? So, we're stuck between feeling optimistic and pessimistic.

Death is a big part of life. Everything eventually dies, no matter how much progress we make or how rich or powerful we become. Death is the end of everything we hold dear - life, beauty, wealth, power, and even virtue. Everyone, whether saint or sinner, king or beggar, faces death. Yet, despite knowing this, we still cling to life. This attachment to life, even though everything ultimately ends in death, is called an illusion.

Think of a mother caring for her child with all her heart. Even if that child grows up to be cruel and abusive, the mother still loves them and makes excuses for their behaviour, calling it love. But deep down, it's not love; it's like something has taken control of her, making it impossible for her to break free from the attachment she feels. This feeling of being unable to let go, even when it's harmful, is an illusion.

We're all chasing after something valuable, like the Golden Fleece from the ancient tales. Even though we know our chances of getting it are slim, we still strive for it. This feeling of pursuing something unreachable is an illusion.

Despite death being a constant presence in our lives, we often believe we'll live forever. King Yudhishthira once said that the most amazing thing on Earth is that people see death happening all the time, yet they still believe they'll never die. This illusion of immortality is an illusion

Knowing happiness also means knowing unhappiness. So, which path should we choose? Even the smallest bit of material wealth we have can cause the same amount of suffering elsewhere. This is a universal law. While young people might not see it clearly, those who have lived longer and faced struggles understand it better.

These things happen all the time, and finding a solution to this problem seems impossible. Why is it like this? It's hard to answer because the question itself doesn't make logical sense. We just know that it happens, and we can't change it. Even understanding it fully is beyond our ability. So, how can we solve it?

Illusion simply states how the universe works. Some people get scared when they hear about these things, but we need to be brave. Ignoring facts won't help. Sometimes, when we're optimistic, it's like a hare hiding its head from danger, but that won't solve anything. Some people object to this, but they often have many good things in life. it's tough to be pessimistic because everyone talks about how great the world is, but everyone's experience is different.

Sometimes we hear that as evolution progresses, evil will be eliminated, leaving only good behind. This idea makes those who have an easy life feel good, but it ignores the suffering of others. It assumes that good and evil are absolute realities and that good is increasing while evil is decreasing. But is it true that evil is decreasing?

As machines make things cheaper and lead to progress, millions suffer so that a few can become rich. While some become wealthy, many become poorer and are even enslaved. This is how things are happening. When people focus only on their senses, their happiness and misery depend on their physical well-being. But as they progress and experience more, their capacity for both happiness and suffering increases. Those who live in simpler conditions may not experience jealousy, legal troubles, taxes, or societal pressure, but as society advances, so do the challenges and suffering.

As people become more refined and educated, their sensitivity to both happiness and suffering increases. While the common man may not be affected much by verbal abuse, a gentleman might be deeply affected by just a word of insult. This suggests that misery grows along with our ability to experience happiness. This doesn't support the idea of continuous improvement as proposed by evolutionists. As we become happier, we also become more vulnerable to suffering. It seems that the more progress we make, the more opportunities for pain and pleasure arise. This is an illusion.

It's a constant contradiction that wherever there's good, there's also evil, and vice versa. Life and death, happiness and sadness, they always go hand in hand. We can't fix this. We might wish for a place where there's only good and no evil, where we only smile and never cry. But that's impossible because the conditions will always be the same. Wherever there's the ability to make us smile, there's also the ability to make us cry. Wherever there's happiness, there's also the potential for misery.

It is only the belief in optimism or pessimism. The world is a mix of good and evil, happiness and misery, and increasing one often means increasing the other. There's no such thing as a perfectly good or bad world because they contradict each other. Good and bad aren't separate; they're just different expressions of the same thing. What seems good today might seem bad tomorrow, and vice versa. To stop evil, we'd have to stop good too. Life without death or happiness without misery isn't possible because they're interconnected. What we consider good or ideal changes over time; what made us happy in the past might not make us happy anymore.

People might question, "What's the purpose of doing good if it consistently entails encountering some negative consequences?" Well, the answer is, that we should still work to reduce suffering because it's the only way to find happiness for ourselves. Sooner or later, everyone realizes this. The smart ones figure it out earlier, and the slower ones take a bit longer. But we all learn eventually. Secondly, we have to keep doing good because it's the only way to break free from this cycle of contradiction. Good and evil will continue to shape our world until we wake up from our illusions and stop chasing temporary pleasures. It might take a while for us to grasp this lesson, but we'll get there eventually.

Everything we experience through our senses, mind, or intellect is limited. Trying to make the limited into the unlimited is impossible and absurd. We can let go of worldly attachments. Even though it's hard to talk about this nowadays, it's the only path to true spirituality. Eventually, the mind awakens from its illusions and desires, realizing that seeking fulfilment through desires only leads to more desires.

All the pleasures we experience through our senses, intellect, and mind are trapped within an illusion, the illusionary network of existence. No matter how much we pursue enjoyment, we end up encountering misery. It's like pouring butter on fire-it only makes it burn more fiercely. This applies to all kinds of enjoyment we seek, whether through our senses or our intellect. It's like being stuck in a maze where we keep running in circles, finding no real satisfaction. When I think about it, I believe that the concept of Illusion, the idea that everything is an illusion, is the best explanation for this cycle of pleasure and pain.

If parents arrange marriages for their children, it often leads to less conflict and more practicality in relationships, but it may lack the romantic element. However, when individuals choose their partners, it doesn't always guarantee happiness. where marriages are often arranged, there's generally less conflict between spouses, and women tend to be content. there's more freedom in choosing partners, many marriages face unhappiness. This suggests that despite our efforts to find happiness, it often comes with its share of unhappiness.

Shouldn't we still strive to do good? Absolutely, but with even more enthusiasm than before. However, this knowledge will help us let go of our extremism. for example, a man will no longer be quick to criticize another but will learn to respect different customs and beliefs. With less extremism, we can focus more on practical work. Extremists waste a lot of energy, but level-headed, calm individuals can work effectively. Understanding the nature of the world will also cultivate patience within us. We'll be less disturbed by misery or evil, knowing that the world is progressing in its way. Even if everyone becomes good, other forms of life like animals and plants will continue to evolve. But one thing is certain: everything is moving towards its ultimate destination, just like a river flowing into the ocean. So, despite life's challenges and joys, we're all moving towards perfection and freedom.

There is nothing pessimism nor optimism. The world is not all evil or not all good. our evil is of no less value than our good, and our good is of no more value than our evil. They are bound together. This is the world, and knowing this, we work with patience.

Everyone, knowingly or unknowingly, feels trapped and wants to break free. Since childhood, we're taught about limits, making us realize we're confined in some way. Even in simple beliefs, like worshipping ancestors, there's this idea of seeking freedom. People see gods as having more freedom than themselves. This idea grows until it reaches the concept of a Personal God, who's seen as beyond all limitations. Imagine ancient sages debating this in a forest, with one young person claiming to have found the answer: knowing a higher power beyond darkness leads to transcending death.

Illusion is everywhere and can be tough to deal with. Nevertheless, we must persevere. Waiting for everything to be perfect before starting is like waiting for a river to dry up before crossing it. Instead of going along with the illusion, we have to go against it. We're not just here to go along with nature but to challenge it.

Look at houses, for example. Nature didn't make them; humans did, even though nature might prefer us to live in forests. Throughout history, humans have been fighting against what nature seems to dictate, and in the end, we usually win. Inside ourselves, there's also a battle between our basic instincts and our higher selves, between darkness and light. But in this battle too, humans often come out victorious, breaking free from nature's constraints.

Some philosophers believe there's something beyond illusion, the illusion that binds us. If we can reach that place, we won't be trapped by illusion anymore. It's just the start of the spiritual journey, not the end. Initially, they talk about a Personal God, the one who controls illusion, but it evolves. Eventually, they realize that the one they thought was outside is actually within themselves. They discover that they are the ones who are truly free, even though they once thought they were bound by limitations.

When we judge others, we often use our standards or beliefs, which isn't fair. Everyone should be judged based on their standards, not ours. Many of our arguments come from this misunderstanding. We assume others' intentions are the same as ours when they act in a certain way, but they might have different reasons altogether. Just because someone does something similar to what we would do doesn't mean they have the same motives. So, when looking at ancient religions or any beliefs, we shouldn't impose our viewpoint onto them.

It might sound strange, but God doesn't change. He's always the same. Similarly, the true essence of each person doesn't change either. However, our understanding of God and ourselves keeps evolving and expanding. We'll later understand that behind every human expression is an unchanging, perfect essence. Our idea of God is like a reflection of this essence, always changing and expanding. As we learn more, it's like we're progressing in understanding. But sometimes, we might misunderstand or lose sight of the truth, which is called retrogression. So, as we grow and learn, our perception of God and ourselves also grows and evolves.

Why is there disharmony and evil in the universe? In the beginning, early religions didn't wonder about this because people back then didn't see the world as full of conflicts. They simply acted on their instincts without thinking much. Similarly, their gods also acted on impulse.

As people's ethical ideas improved, they began to struggle with their impulses. There's a part of our minds that says "do" and another part that says "don't." One part pushes us to act, while the other urges us to hold back. Normally, our actions are guided by the impulse to move forward. But religion starts with the impulse to turn inward, to say "don't." This impulse is crucial for spirituality to begin. When we have this sense of restraint, it helps our ideas to grow, even though we may have worshipped gods who encouraged fighting in the past.

A small feeling of love started to grow in people's hearts. At first, it was just within tribes, where each tribe worshipped its god, believing the god protected them. Some even thought they were descended from these gods, or the Sun and the Moon. As these ideas developed, people began to feel a sense of duty towards each other and started organizing society a bit. They realized they couldn't live together without being patient and tolerant of each other. So, the idea of restraint came about. Society is built on this idea, and we all know that those who haven't learned to be patient and tolerant lead very unhappy lives.

When new religious ideas emerged, people started thinking about something higher and more moral. The old gods, who were rowdy, aggressive, and enjoyed drinking and eating meat, didn't seem right anymore. Sometimes, they even behaved foolishly. People began questioning their motives and actions, and when they couldn't find good reasons, they stopped worshipping them. Instead, they kept the qualities of the gods that made sense and combined them into one being called the God of gods. This new god wasn't just powerful; he was ethical and cared about people. People thought of him as the most moral and powerful being in the universe.

But all these attempts to explain didn't work. As people tried to understand God better, the problem of evil and suffering seemed even bigger. Why would a powerful and loving God allow such terrible things to happen? Why is there more misery than happiness, and more wickedness than goodness in the world? We might try to ignore these questions, but the truth is, that the world can be an awful place. It's like constantly reaching for something just out of our grasp. We have big ideas and desires, but we struggle to achieve them, and life often knocks us down. If we give up on our ideals and just try to get by, we become like animals and degrade ourselves. Neither way leads to happiness. Those who accept the world as it is are unhappy, and those who strive for truth and higher ideals often face even more misery.

It's a fact that our world feels like a never-ending struggle, like being stuck in a never-ending cycle of desire and disappointment. We don't understand much about the universe, but at the same time, we can't say we know nothing. It's like we're always stuck between knowing and not knowing, in a hazy place where truth and falsehood mix. It's like we're all walking through a dream, sometimes awake, sometimes asleep, never quite sure which is which. This is the reality for all of us, whether we're talking about everyday life, philosophy, or science. This constitutes the reality of our existence.

Whether we call it matter, spirit, mind, or anything else, the truth remains the same: we can't say for sure if they exist or not, if they're one or many. It's like a constant dance between light and darkness, always there but hard to grasp. This is what we call Illusion. We're born into it, live in it, and even our thoughts and dreams are part of it. We can be philosophers, spiritual beings, or even act like devils or gods within Illusion. No matter how big our ideas are, even if they are part of an illusion. Everything we know is just our way of trying to understand Illusion as it appears to us. It's all about names and forms. Anything that has a shape or triggers a thought is part of an illusion because anything bound by time, space, and cause-and-effect is just an illusion.

Let's look back at the early ideas of God and see what happened to them. People started to realize that the idea of a Being who is always loving, unselfish, and all-powerful couldn't explain everything. Philosophers pondered, "Where does the fairness of a benevolent deity lie?" Witnessing millions of beings perish daily to sustain others' lives. Every breath we take, every move we make, and every bite we eat means death for countless beings. Why do they have to die? Some say it's because they're lesser beings, but even if that's true, shouldn't they have a right to live? After all, if they're lowly, shouldn't they have even more reason to live?

Animals experience pleasure and pain much more intensely than humans do because their souls are mainly focused on their senses. They can enjoy things in ways we can't even imagine, but they also suffer greatly. When they die, their pain is even worse than ours, but we often don't think about that when we kill them. This is the illusion that blinds us to the suffering of others. If we believe in a personal God who made everything, the explanations that say good can come from evil aren't enough. Why should good things have to come from evil? If that is true, I could justify hurting others just to satisfy my own desires, and that's not right. The question remains unanswered.

We have always cherished the idea of freedom, which is crucial for progress. If we don't give freedom, things won't improve. The belief that we can control and guide others' growth while keeping our freedom is wrong and harmful. It has held back millions of people. Let everyone have the freedom to choose. That's the only way we can grow and improve.

From the very first moment, man desired freedom. But from that very moment, he was told what freedom is, thereby losing his sense of freedom and ultimately losing it altogether.

Freedom has played a vital role in the development of sciences. In societies, we'll often find two groups of opinions: one that criticizes and condemns, and the other that offers constructive solutions. It's interesting that in every society, when there's a problem, there's always a group that angrily denounces it, sometimes becoming extreme.

Others had compassion in their hearts and understood the importance of addressing the root cause of problems; these were the great saints. It's essential to remember that all the great teachers of the world have stated that they came not to destroy but to fulfil. Unfortunately, this hasn't always been understood, and their patience has been mistaken for weakness.

We couldn't grasp the immense power of love in the hearts of these wise sages, who saw all people as their children. They were our true fathers, filled with boundless sympathy and patience for everyone, guiding them gently upward step by step. They recognized that the old ideas of God didn't align with the advanced ethical concepts of their time. They also acknowledged that atheists often spoke truths, but they understood that those who wanted to uproot society and build anew would ultimately fail.

We don't create entirely new things; we just rearrange what already exists. Like a seed growing into a tree, change happens gradually and naturally. Our focus should be on discovering and fulfilling the truth that already exists, rather than trying to create new truths. Instead of rejecting old ideas about God as outdated, ancient sages sought to understand the underlying reality within them.

Society keeps looking for happiness where it's not, even though they've been told it's pointless. But we can only really understand this through our own experiences. Even when life hits us hard, we often don't learn. Like moths drawn to a flame, we keep chasing pleasure, hoping it'll make us happy. We keep coming back, only to end up hurt and unsatisfied. It's all an illusion.

Every breath, every heartbeat, every move-we feel free, yet we're constantly reminded we're not. We're slaves to nature, in body, mind, thoughts, and feelings. It's all an illusion.

Illusions and societal messages often lead us to believe that following a certain path will bring us peace. However, when we return disappointed, we tend to blame the rest we once had.

INFUSION

"The old cannot be destroyed, and the new cannot be denied. Therefore, it is the fusion of both that brings balance."

As for the usefulness or outcome of this knowledge, in today's world, everything is judged by its utility or how much money it brings. But who has the right to expect truth to be measured by these standards? If something lacks utility, does that make it less true? Utility isn't the measure of truth. However, there's great usefulness in understanding this truth. Everyone seeks happiness, but most look for it in temporary, fleeting things. True happiness isn't found in sensory pleasures; it's found in connecting with the Spirit within us.

People want to be happy, so they chase after things they think will make them happy. When someone is young and doing well, they believe their success is real. But as they get older and struggle to find happiness, they might blame fate. Eventually, they realize they can't always get what they want. No matter what they do, they face obstacles they can't overcome. Everything they experience-whether it's good or bad-doesn't last forever. Happiness, sadness, having lots of money or none at all, power, and even life itself, all come and go.

There are two ways people think about the world. Some believe in nihilism, which says everything is meaningless and we can't know anything about the past, future, or even the present. But it's hard for anyone to truly believe in nothingness because it means denying everything, even basic things like family. The other way is to search for meaning and truth in the constantly changing world. Throughout history, people have tried to find what's real, even beyond our physical bodies. They look for something completer and more perfect, something that lasts even when our bodies don't.

People have a dream about a time called the "Age of Truth." They imagine it as a perfect time when nobody dies unless they want to, and they can keep their bodies healthy for as long as they want. There was no evil or sadness. They believe that the present time is just a corrupted version of that perfect past. Many religions have stories about a big flood that wiped out a lot of people, which they see as proof that the world got worse over time. But they believe that slowly, things are getting better again, and one day, we'll reach that perfect state again.

Why do people believe in religion, God, and the search for the afterlife? It's because deep down, within ourselves, there's a longing for something perfect. We search for this ideal in various places, but in the end, we realize that the perfection we seek is actually within us. After searching everywhere, we come back to ourselves and discover that the ultimate truth we've been seeking is our own inner self. we don't need to become pure or perfect because we already are. Nature is like a screen hiding this truth, and every good thought or action we take removes a piece of that screen, revealing the purity, infinity, and divine essence within us.

Throughout history, humanity has been gradually uncovering the truth about our existence. As we peel away the layers of ignorance, more of the light within us shines through, because it's the nature of that light to shine. However, this truth is beyond knowing. If it were knowable, it wouldn't be what it is, because it's the eternal subject, the witness of everything in the universe, including ourselves.

The biggest problem is ignorance, especially the mistaken belief that we are limited beings, separate from each other and the Infinite. This ignorance leads to selfishness and misery. If even a small fraction of people could let go of selfishness and narrow-mindedness, the world would be a much better place. But relying solely on material progress won't achieve this. Without spiritual knowledge, material advancements only worsen the situation, empowering selfish individuals to exploit others instead of helping them.

Another question people ask is, "Is it practical? Can these spiritual truths be practised in modern society?" The truth remains indifferent to the opinions of society, regardless of whether they are ancient or contemporary. Society needs to honour the truth, or it will perish. Societies should be built on truth, not the other way around. If noble truths like unselfishness can't be practised in society, it's better for people to leave society and live in the forest. That's true courage.

There are two kinds of courage: one is facing physical danger, like facing a cannon, and the other is having the courage of spiritual conviction. An Emperor once met a sage and tried to convince him to come to his country. But the sage refused, saying he was content in his forest. Even when the emperor threatened to kill him, the sage remained calm, knowing that nothing could harm his eternal spirit. This is true spiritual boldness, different from the courage of a lion or tiger facing physical danger.

What's the point of boasting about the strength of our muscles or the greatness of our society if we can't align it with the truth? If we can't create a society where the highest truths are put into practice, then what's the use of all this talk? Is money the only practical thing? If so, why brag about our society? The greatest society is one where the highest truths are lived out. If society isn't ready for the highest truth, then change it, and the sooner, the better. Stand up, people, and believe in truth, and practice it boldly! The world needs courageous individuals who dare to live by truth, who aren't afraid of death but welcome it because they know they are eternal spirits. Then we will be truly free, and we'll understand our real essence.

In modern times, there's a tendency to focus too much on doing work and not enough on thinking. But doing work comes from thinking. When we fill our minds with high thoughts and ideals, great work comes out of it. Instead of talking about impurity, we should affirm our purity. We've convinced ourselves that we're small and mortal, living in constant fear.

We see wickedness because our perceptions shape how we view the world. For example, imagine mistaking a stump of a tree for different things in the dark, like a thief or a ghost. Similarly, if there's a baby in a room with stolen gold, it wouldn't recognize it as stolen because it has no concept of theft. Rather than focusing on the world's wickedness and sins, we should lament that we're forced to witness such things. Instead of condemning and weakening the world further, we should teach people, even from a young age, that they are all glorious and strong, children of immortality. Let positive, strong, and helpful thoughts fill their minds.

The small fish desires to flee its aquatic predators. How does it manage? By sprouting wings and transforming into a bird. Notably, the fish doesn't alter the water or air; the transformation occurs internally. Change, fundamentally, is a personal endeavour. Throughout evolution, the conquest of nature arises from inner transformation. This concept applies to faith and morality, where triumph over evil stems from internal change.

Faith begins when we have a genuine realization in our souls. At that point, true morality emerges. If society suddenly allowed stealing without consequences, we'd likely indulge in it. It's social norms and consequences that keep us in check, not some inherent morality. Deep down, we know this truth about ourselves. Let's admit we're not as religious as we pretend to be and refrain from judging others. We'll truly embody morality when we've embraced religion and recognized our shared humanity.

In the past, people lived in forests and resorted to cannibalism, while today, cheating and deception plague modern society, leading to ruin on a grand scale. This doesn't signify progress but rather an increase in desires. Desires are the root cause of all misery, perpetuating a cycle of longing and dissatisfaction. As the ability to fulfil desires grows, so does the intensity of desire itself. Therefore, happiness gained by one often results in suffering for another. Human population growth and the exploitation of animals for resources further compound this imbalance. Consequently, the notion of this world becoming a paradise, either practically or theoretically, seems unfounded.

Desire leads to suffering. If we have no desires, we won't suffer, but we won't evolve either. Even though suffering teaches us lessons, there's also glory in happiness and even in suffering.

Desire a long and fulfilling life, but let your desires be noble, aimed at serving others and finding joy in your actions. By living this way, you'll discover the path to enlightenment. If one indulges blindly in worldly pleasures without seeking truth, they lose their way and miss the ultimate goal.

In life, happiness and sadness go hand in hand, just like life and death. They're not separate; they're different aspects of the same thing. Good and evil aren't distinct entities; they're just different degrees of the same reality. Sometimes what brings pleasure to one person causes pain to another. Eating meat may bring pleasure to a person, yet it inflicts pain upon the animal being consumed. There exists no pleasure that universally satisfies all individuals. Some are pleased, others displeased. So, on it will go. Life isn't about having only good things without any bad. It might be disappointing to hear, but until proven otherwise, that's how it is.

In life, happiness and sadness are like two sides of the same coin. Similarly, life and death, joy and sorrow, good and evil-they're all part of the same reality. They're not separate, but different expressions of the same thing. While some may see them as opposites, they're actually just varying degrees of intensity.

For example, our nerves transmit both pleasant and painful sensations. If a nerve is damaged, we lose both types of sensation. Similarly, a person's level of happiness or misery depends on their circumstances. A primitive person finds happiness in simple pleasures, while someone with more knowledge enjoys intellectual pursuits. As people evolve intellectually, they become more susceptible to mental pain, which the primitive mind doesn't experience.

Despite the idea that good and evil may be decreasing over time, history shows that both are continuously present and evolving.

We shouldn't teach children that the world is all good, like a paradise filled with flowers and honey. That's just a dream. But it's also wrong to think everything is bad just because someone suffers more than others. Life is a mix of good and evil experiences. Good and evil aren't separate; they're the same thing, just showing up in different ways and intensities, creating different feelings in our minds.

First, let us take charge of ourselves, break free, and go beyond the limits of these laws. They don't completely control us, they're just a part of who we are. Realize that we're not a slave to nature, we never are and never will be. our soul is vast like an ocean, while nature is just a small part of it. we're greater than the stars, the sun, and the moon; they're like tiny bubbles compared to our infinite essence. Once we understand this, we'll be able to master both good and evil. Then, we'll see the world differently and appreciate both the beauty of goodness and the wonder of evil.

We create our own suffering, we define what's good and what's evil, and we're the one who covers our eyes and thinks it's dark. Remove our hands and see the light we're radiant, we're already perfect from the start.

Since everyone has different ideas about happiness and pleasure, what brings joy to one person may cause pain to another. Therefore, there can't be one single existing heaven that satisfies everybody universally. The highest heaven is within ourselves - the human soul is the greatest temple of worship, surpassing all heavens. In no external realm can we understand reality as clearly as within our own souls? Moving from place to place doesn't offer much help in this pursuit. We create our own worlds, so if I'm evil, everything seems evil to me. This applies to all realms; even if I go to heaven after death, it'll be the same until I become pure. It's pointless to run around seeking truth externally. Immortality is gained by seeing with the pure mind, not with physical eyes.

When we dedicate our work to God, we become free from the bondage of its effects. False desires cause suffering, but when purified through divine dedication, they no longer bring evil or misery. Those unaware of this truth remain trapped in a world of ignorance. Many have yet to discover the infinite bliss within and around them, living instead in a world clouded by ignorance.

Despite being surrounded by abundance; we remain thirsty beside a mighty river and hungry near heaps of food. The blissful universe is ever-present, yet we fail to recognize it. The universe aims to reveal this truth to us, as the longing for this blissful existence resides in every heart.

Talking about seeing God everywhere is easy, but when we face challenges in the world, that idea disappears. For instance, while walking on the street, we believe God is in every person, but when someone pushes us, we quickly forget that notion and react angrily. Instead of seeing God, we see negativity. We should immerse ourselves in noble thoughts until they become part of us, shaping our actions and words. Thoughts drive us forward, so let's fill our minds with the highest ideals, hearing and pondering them consistently. Failure is natural and essential, for it adds depth and meaning to life. Embrace struggles and mistakes as part of life's poetry.

Animals never lie they don't evolve either, but humans do. Yet, don't be discouraged by failures or setbacks. Keep striving for the ideal, even if you fail many times. Aim to see God in everything, but if that's difficult, start by seeing Him in something you love. Gradually expand your vision. There's endless opportunity for spiritual growth. Be patient, and you'll reach your goal.

Nature works in cycles. Just like a tiny seed grows into a big tree and then returns to being a seed again, everything in nature follows a similar pattern. Birds hatch from eggs, which are like seeds for future birds. This cycle repeats in animals and humans too. Everything starts from simple forms and gradually becomes more complex before returning to its original form. For example, raindrops evaporate from the ocean, turn into clouds, and then fall back to earth as rain, only to evaporate again. Mountains are constantly shaped by glaciers and rivers, breaking down into sand that eventually forms new mountains. This cycle of creation and destruction is a fundamental aspect of nature.

Creation follows a rhythm of rising and falling waves, just like breathing. Everything in the universe, including the sun, moon, stars, and earth, returns to its finer causes and eventually re-emerges in new forms. Similarly, just as a seed needs time underground before sprouting, creation undergoes a cycle of degeneration and regeneration.

They say God is like a magnet, and the human soul is like a needle. The soul gets covered in dirt and dust from its bad actions. When the soul becomes pure, it naturally moves towards God and stays with Him forever, though still separate. A perfected soul can take any form it wants or even have nobody at all. It becomes very powerful, except it can't create like God can. No matter how perfect, souls can't control the universe; that's God's job. But all perfected souls become forever happy and live eternally with God.

Some people believe in asking God for material things like "Give me this and give me that." If someone needs something material, they should ask higher beings like gods, angels, or perfected beings. Others think God should only be loved; it's almost disrespectful to ask God for material things. According to them, if you want something material, you can pray to one of the gods, but if you want salvation, you should worship God.

When we let go of our selfish desires, we transcend mortality and become one with God, even while living on earth. By freeing ourselves from the entanglements of the heart, we experience the divine presence here and now, not elsewhere.

Some people believe everything is predetermined by a higher power, and we must accept it without question. They think our actions, experiences, and suffering are all predestined, and we should endure hardships quietly. They follow these beliefs because ancient texts say so.

Some may find the idea of breaking free from superstitions daunting, but that's just because we've been conditioned to believe in them since childhood. Just as some people feel scared in the dark despite not believing in ghosts, many can't imagine religion without the concept of the devil. We've grown accustomed to being told what to do and being reprimanded, but it's all just superstition. Eventually, we'll look back and laugh at how these beliefs held us back from realizing our true, pure selves.

God's mercy extends to everyone, regardless of their actions or beliefs. He doesn't play favourites or punish us for our mistakes. Blaming God for our suffering is futile; we must take responsibility for our own actions and strive to do better. Blaming others only weakens us further. Instead, we should accept our faults, stand tall, and shape our destiny. The past has departed, but the future remains within our power to shape. Every word, thought, and action contributes to our future, so let's focus on nurturing positivity and goodness within ourselves.

We've become weak and dependent, always seeking support from others. Many people prefer a religion that makes them feel good rather than seeking the truth. Only a few dare to learn and follow the truth in their daily lives. It's not their fault; it's just a weakness of the mind. When a new, profound idea comes along, it can shake things up in our minds and cause disruption. This can throw people off balance because they're used to their familiar surroundings and beliefs. They have to overcome a lot of old superstitions—ones passed down through families, communities, and cultures, as well as the natural tendency in all of us to believe in superstitions. But there are still a few courageous people who are willing to embrace and pursue the truth, no matter what.

Humans are the ones who shape the fate of humanity. The bad things in the world are our fault. We create evil, and the suffering we see is often because of the bad things we've done in the past. So, according to this idea, humans are the ones who are responsible, not God. It's like the saying goes, "We get what we give."

Some believe that beyond our world, there's a place of pure happiness and goodness. They think once we reach that place, we won't have to be born and die anymore. There, there's no sickness or death, only eternal happiness with God. They believe all beings, from the smallest creatures to the highest gods, will eventually reach this place of bliss. Our world, however, keeps going forever in cycles, without ever ending.

Some believe that they have no right to take any life because they see everything as belonging to God. So, when they're asked why they don't harm animals, they say it's because everything belongs to the Lord, not to them. They believe that when a person reaches a state where they don't claim ownership over anything when they love everyone and are willing to sacrifice their life for an animal, they have truly surrendered to God.

If we consider that after death, good people enjoy heaven before coming back to Earth, while the wicked become ghosts or demons before becoming animals. Eventually, they get another chance to be human and improve themselves. Earth is where our actions determine our future after death. So, whatever the truth is, humans have the best chance to become perfect because they're the highest beings in the universe. Even angels or gods have to become human to reach perfection. Human life is where we have the best opportunity to grow and improve.

Our eyes are just tools for seeing, not the actual organs of vision. Even if we have many eyes, we can't see. The same goes for our other senses like hearing. Just having the tools and organs isn't enough; our mind needs to be paying attention too.

We see what we want to see and we see from our perception and hear from our beliefs.

If everyone here had the same thoughts, we wouldn't have any thoughts to think. We understand that it takes different ideas to come together to create movement. When thoughts clash and differ, that's when we start thinking.

We all see truth differently based on where we come from, what we've learned, and our surroundings. We understand the truth with our hearts and minds, but we can only know as much as our circumstances allow. This leads to different ideas among people, but we're all part of the same truth.

People are trying to make peace in society, but it's really hard. Life is tough, and people feel stressed out. Making peace inside ourselves is even harder.

We've all heard about love, peace, and being fair since we were kids. But now, those words don't mean much to many of us. They're just things we say without thinking. Some really wise people came up with those words, and back then, people really got what they meant. But now, people just use those words to sound good.

Every development has an initial stage. Like how machines need energy put into them to work, humans also have a starting point. If we evolved from simpler creatures, then the potential for greatness was already within those simpler beings. This helps us understand ancient teachings in a modern context. The energy that drives us needs something beyond itself to control it. This is where the idea of the soul comes in. The soul works through a subtle body, which then influences the physical body. Each person has their own soul and subtle body, guiding their actions through the mind and body.

When people stop dwelling on the past or worrying about the future, and when they let go of the idea of their bodies because bodies come and go, they reach a higher understanding. The real essence of a person isn't their body or mind, which are always changing. Every particle in the body is constantly changing, and the mind is like a whirlpool of ever-shifting thoughts and emotions. But the true essence, or Spirit, is beyond change because change can only happen to limited things.

The universe as a whole is unchangeable and absolute. Our true reality lies in being part of this universal essence, not in our limited selves. It might be scary to think of ourselves as part of something vast and everywhere, but in reality, everything we do, every movement, every word, and every feeling, is a manifestation of this universal essence working through us.

People get scared when they hear this because they worry about losing their sense of individuality. But what is individuality? If it's in the body, then things like growing a beard or losing a hand would mean losing individuality. But that doesn't make sense. Changing habits or becoming a better person doesn't mean losing individuality either. Individuality isn't in our memories either, because if we forget something, it's like it never happened. So, the only real individuality is in the infinite, unchanging essence of who we are. Everything else is always changing.

We're not truly individuals yet. We're working towards becoming individuals, and that means connecting with the infinite essence of who we are. Only when we live our lives for the whole universe, and for others, do we truly live.

The real individual, or Spirit, is infinite and undivided. Evolution isn't about the Spirit changing; it's about the Spirit gradually revealing itself through nature. Just like a screen with a small hole that grows larger, revealing more of what's behind it, our true selves are gradually revealed through evolution. We're already perfect and free; we just need to realize it.

Focusing on limited things speeds up our journey towards death. The fear of death disappears when we realize that as long as there's life in the universe, we're alive. When we feel connected to everything and everyone, we become fearless. Immortality doesn't make sense in a world of constant change.

INNER PEACE

"Authentic peace arises from within, embraced by the soul, transforming into a lasting essence we term inner peace."

Knowledge, in a way, limits this understanding because it objectifies things. But in reality, we are already that eternal subject, and we're constantly trying to express it in different ways. This is why there are so many ethical codes and ideas about doing good to others. The essence of all ethical systems is the idea of helping others, whether they're humans or animals. This stems from the realization that we are all connected, that the universe is one. Even the hardest hearts can feel sympathy for others because deep down, we all share the same essence.

Even if someone feels uneasy hearing that their sense of individuality is not as real as they think, they still agree that extreme selflessness is crucial for morality. Perfect self-abnegation means letting go of the idea of "me and mine," which is just a leftover belief from the past. The more we release this notion of a separate self, the more our true Self shines through. This is the core of moral teaching, and whether people realize it or not, the world is gradually moving towards it, even if most are doing it unconsciously. But if we consciously embrace this truth, understanding that our sense of self is just a limitation, we can truly embody our infinite nature.

The light that shines through borrowed sources fades, unlike the inherent and unchanging light. Just as the moon waxes and wanes with the sun's borrowed light, external forms lack self-luminosity. True luminosity belongs to the unchanging and self-luminous soul, not the fluctuating body and mind. The soul is not just knowledgeable, existent, or happy; it is knowledge, existence, and happiness itself. We understand that a human comprises the outer shell, the body, followed by the subtler body containing the mind, intellect, and ego. Behind them lies the true Self. All the attributes and capabilities of the physical body originate from the mind, while the mind, in turn, derives its abilities and radiance from the soul, which stands as its foundation.

People have asked many questions about the soul, which is said to be neither the body nor the mind. Different philosophies agree that the soul has no specific form or shape, so it must be everywhere, or omnipresent. Since time, space, and causation are concepts in the mind, and the soul is beyond the mind and formless, it must also be beyond these concepts. This means it's infinite. And if it's infinite, there can only be one soul, not separate souls for each person. So, the real essence of each person is one infinite spirit, while the individual identities we see are just limitations of that one spirit.

In a way, myths are true when they say that the people, we see are just faint reflections of the real, greater beings beyond. The real essence, or Spirit, is beyond cause and effect, not limited by time or space, so it's free. The individuals we see are limited by time, space, and cause and effect, or karma, so they seem bound. But in reality, they're not really bound. This spiritual nature is within us, making us infinite, so there's no real birth or death for the soul.

We never go far from the soul. When all life and the whole universe are seen in this soul, then alone man has attained the secret. There is no more delusion for us. Where is any more misery for us, when we see this Oneness in the universe?

There's a story about a lioness who gave birth while trying to attack a flock of sheep. She died, and her baby lion was raised by the sheep, growing up thinking it was one of them. Even when it became a full-grown lion, it still believed it was a sheep. Another lion tried to convince it otherwise, but it refused to believe until it saw its reflection in a lake and realized it was a lion. Similarly, we are like lions, pure, infinite, and perfect souls. There's no need to cry or fear, as we are eternal and untouched by birth or death, like the infinite sky that remains unchanged despite passing clouds. The truth we've sought was always within us, yet in our ignorance, we believed we'd lost it. We searched far and wide, unaware that it resided in our hearts all along. That's where we must look to find it.

God, nature, and the soul are all connected.

Think of God as the Soul, and nature and souls as God's body. Just like I have a body and a soul, the whole universe and all souls are like God's body, and God is the Soul within them. So, God is the reason the universe exists. The body may change be young or old, strong or weak but that doesn't affect the soul. It's always the same, eternal existence, showing itself through the body.

Bodies come and go, but the soul stays the same. Likewise, the whole universe is like God's body, so in that way, it's God. But changes in the universe don't change God. From this material, God creates the universe. At the end of a cycle, His body becomes finer, then expands again at the start of a new cycle, giving rise to different worlds.

God is both the creator and the creation of the universe. He appears to become the universe itself. In reality, what we see as the universe is just an illusion. Everything, including ourselves, is a part of the Infinite Existence, the soul. The true essence is beyond names and forms. If we remove these differences, everything is one. There is no distinction between nature, God, or the universe; there is only the Infinite Existence. We can't fully understand this essence; we can only reflect upon it. The universe is like a reflection of the Eternal Being, the soul, and our actions determine the quality of this reflection.

God controls everything in nature, from the sky to the air to the sun. He is the essence of reality and the soul within us. When we see things as two, we feel fear, danger, and conflict. But when we realize everything is one, there's no one to hate or fight. This understanding reveals the true nature of life and perfection, which is God. Seeing the oneness frees us from delusion and brings blessings. Ideas of being a man, woman, sick, healthy, strong, weak, hating, loving, or having power are illusions. Recognizing our oneness with God makes us strong and fearless. Any thought or word weakening us is the only evil. Nothing can frighten us because we are indestructible like a rock. We are the essence, the divine force within the cosmos.

It's foolish and wicked to believe we are sinners when we are all God. Don't sit and weep over such nonsense. When someone inflicts harm upon us, it's akin to harming our own selves. When we help others, let's not feel proud; it's our duty, not a reason for pride. The entire universe is us; everything is an expression of our essence. So, who would we hate or fight? We should Know that we are God and live our life accordingly. Those who understand and live by this truth will no longer dwell in darkness.

In this universe, both change and things don't change. The body, mind, and soul are actually one, even though they seem separate. Someone who sees the body doesn't see the mind or soul, and someone who sees the mind doesn't see the soul. But for someone who sees the soul, the body and mind don't exist. It's comparable to mistaking a rope for a snake. When the illusion ends, the snake disappears, and all that's left is the rope.

There's only one existence that appears in many forms. This Self or Soul is everything in the universe. It's like waves in the sea - each wave seems separate because of its name and shape, but really, they're all part of the same sea.

When someone cries out for help from above the skies, they don't realize that the skies are within them too. They seek help externally, but it actually comes from within themselves. Like a sick person who hears a tap on the door, only to find it's just their own heartbeat. Similarly, after searching for gods outside themselves, people eventually realize that the true God is their own Self. "I am He, and He is I." There's only one God, and it's within us all along.

The illusion comes from itself. When we see the truth, the illusion goes away. It relies on its own tricks, not on God or the soul. You're not stuck in an illusion; it's just there. Like clouds in the sky, they come and go, but the sky stays blue. You're naturally pure and perfect. You're like the universe itself, and there's only one-no "you and I," just "I."

First, people believed in a personal God outside the universe. Then, they realized God was within the universe. Finally, they understood that the soul itself is one with God, connecting all the different parts of the universe. In today's society, all three stages are necessary and each one leads to the next. Everyone should follow their own beliefs about the universe. Don't harm anyone, respect where they are, and help them if you can. Eventually, everyone will reach the truth. When desires fade, mortals become immortal, and ordinary people become divine.

The universe appears as matter to our senses, as souls to our intellect, and as God to our spirit. For someone covered in veils of wickedness, the universe seems ugly. For someone seeking enjoyment, it appears as heaven. But for the perfect person, it all disappears, merging into their Self.

In the Oneness of life, in this unity of everything, we discover that all our misery stems from ignorance. This ignorance is the belief in separateness, the idea of division between man and man, nation and nation, and even between objects like the earth and the moon, or the sun and the moon. This separation is not real; it is only an illusion on the surface. Deep down, there is unity between all beings and things. Those who understand this Oneness have no more delusion. They see the reality of everything, the secret of existence. In this reality, there is no death, no sorrow, no misery only perfect union and bliss. They have transcended the limitations of the material world and attained eternal bliss.

The soul is connected to freedom, existence, and knowledge. It's like a deep, inner sense of being alive and aware. This essence is filled with bliss. Birth, death, and everything in between are just different ways this essence shows itself. Whether we're as small as a worm or as brilliant as a genius, we all have this essence within us. Various spiritual beliefs, talk about regaining this inner state of bliss. They say it's not about gaining something new, but remembering what's already ours. We're like kings who forgot their kingdom and need to reclaim it. Some say we never lost it; it's just an illusion.

Different spiritual teachings offer various ways to regain our inner sense of completeness, like performing rituals, asking for forgiveness, or loving a higher being. However, the ultimate advice is that we don't need to do anything because we never truly lose our inner freedom and purity. If we believe we're free, we are, and if we think we're bound, we are. This might sound bold, but it's true. If freedom isn't our nature, we can't attain it, and if we lose it, we never had it in the first place.

We're not bound; we're already free. Thinking or saying we're bound is dangerous, it's like hypnotizing ourselves. The faith that focuses on a Personal God can be comforting, but it can also make us dependent and weak in the long run. What the world needs now is strength, not weakness. Weakness is the root of suffering and all the problems we face. When we let go of weakness and delusion, everything changes. It's as simple as that.

If the soul is naturally pure and free, then nothing in the universe can bind it. If the soul can attain freedom, it must be because it's inherently free. Freedom means being independent from external influences. If the soul is truly free, it can't be affected by anything and can't die. So, freedom, immortality, and happiness all rely on the soul being beyond external influences and illusion.

True faith remains constant. It's not mere discourse, doctrine, or beautiful theories, but rather, an awakening. It's about transformation, not just hearing or acknowledging. It's the complete evolution of the soul into what it believes. That, indeed, is true spirituality."

The soul is beyond gender. Enlightened beings see everyone as divine. All beings are the same pure essence; only outer appearances differ. The universe is one, with no separation. We can't directly know the essence of the self, only reflect on it. The universe is like a reflection of this essence, and its quality depends on individual purity. There's only one eternal soul in the universe, unaffected by birth, death, or reincarnation. Ideas of heaven and earth are just creations of the mind.

Let us Open our minds to these empowering thoughts instead of weakening ones. Repeat to ourselves, "I am the Universe, I am the Universe" like the constant ringing of a bell. The strength of the world is within us. Cast away the superstitions that cloud our minds. Let's be courageous. Understand the truth and live by it. The goal may seem far, but stay awake, rise, and don't stop until we reach it.

The divine presence transitions from the heavens to nature, then within ourselves. The ultimate truth is that what we've sought externally resides within us. Our true nature is freedom, and illusion never truly binds us. Once we realize this deeply, all difficulties fade, and life transforms into a beautiful playground. Even challenges and suffering reveal their true nature as manifestations of the divine self.

We no longer blame nature or call the world awful and pointless. Once we understand the reasons behind struggle, competition, and even cruelty, we see they're part of life's journey. They push us toward our destined path, even if we don't realize it. Everything in nature, including us, is striving for freedom, moving towards a common goal.

Each person has three parts: the body, the mind, and the soul, which is the true self. The body and mind surround the soul, which is immaterial and immortal. Unlike the body and mind, the soul doesn't follow the laws of cause and effect and has no beginning or end.

Our actions shape our character. These actions influence our direction after death. Even after the body dies, the character remains, guiding the mind until it dissolves, leading to freedom. Our struggle in life resembles a caterpillar building a cocoon with its own actions. The ultimate goal is freedom, where the soul realizes its omnipresence and breaks free from the cycle of birth and death.

Our minds are like vessels, each striving to understand God. Just as water fills different vessels, the perception of God varies for each individual. Despite these differences, God remains singular, present in every form. This acknowledgement of universality is fundamental.

It's hard to find universality in the world of differences, but we know it is there. We're all humans, but are we all the same? No way. Only a crazy person would say that. Are we all equally smart, strong, or talented? Nope, some of us are better at stuff than others. We made these differences because we have different abilities. But still, the idea of fairness matters to us. We're all human, after all.

Despite our diverse appearances black or white, woman or man, we all share a common humanity. Likewise, a universal spirituality, embodied by God, permeates through various religions. Unity amidst diversity is intrinsic to existence. While differences persist in our expressions, we are ultimately unified in the divine. However, expecting uniformity in beliefs, myths, or rituals is impractical and would diminish the richness of life, which flourishes through diversity and balance.

We shouldn't desire uniformity of thought, for then there would be no room for new ideas. Imagine us all alike, resembling statues in a museum, gazing at each other without a single thought to stir. It's our differences, our unique perspectives, that drive progress and ignite thought. This diversity must always be celebrated.

We must understand that the same thing can be perceived from countless perspectives and yet remain unchanged. Consider the sun: as a man journeys towards it, photographing each stage, the images vary, but it's the same sun captured at different points. Similarly, in our quest for the Divine, whether through philosophy, mythology, ritualism, or fetishism, every sect and soul is striving towards God. Every truth we perceive is a glimpse of Him. Imagine we all fetch water from a lake with different vessels a cup, a jar, a bucket. The water conforms to the shape of each vessel, but it's still water. Similarly, our perceptions of the Divine may vary, but the essence remains the same.

Each of us naturally grows and develops according to our nature; eventually, we come to know the highest truth. Ultimately, individuals must educate themselves. What can you or I do? Can we even teach a child? No, the child teaches themselves. We must provide opportunities and remove obstacles. Like a plant growing, you don't make the plant grow; your duty is to protect it from harm. The spiritual growth of every individual follows a similar path. No one can teach you or make you spiritual. You have to educate yourself; your growth must come from within.

Respect others' beliefs, refrain from destructive actions, and offer assistance when feasible. Instead of criticizing, guide individuals forward from where they stand. Eventually, all paths converge towards unity, leading us to a common centre where differences dissolve.

When you take away names and shapes, everything is the same. It's like the ocean; can you tell where one wave ends and the ocean begins? The universe is like that too – it's all one thing, but we see it as many because of names and shapes. Imagine sunlight shining on lots of water droplets; each one reflects the sun, but they all look different. Similarly, the one soul, the one existence of the universe, reflects differently in everything. There's no real "me" or "you" – it's all just one. Thinking there are two is a mistake. When we realize there's only one, we see that we are the universe itself.

The wave and the sea differ because of their form. When the wave disappears, its form vanishes too. The wave exists because of the sea, but the sea doesn't rely on the wave. This idea of form is called illusion. Illusion isn't real because it depends on something else to exist. But it's important because it creates diversity. The illusion comes from one infinite existence, showing us many things. In reality, there's only one substance. Thinking there are two realities is a mistake. When we understand there's only one, we're correct. We see this truth in everyday life and spiritual experiences.

Nature is like a book for the soul, with each chapter unfolding one after another. Scenes come and go, but the soul remains eternal and unchanged. Birth and death happen in nature, not in the soul. However, many people are fooled by this, just like how we used to think the sun moved around the Earth. Birth and death are like illusions, similar to thinking the fields move instead of the train. Different people may see reality differently based on their state of mind and existence.

You, me, the sun, the moon, and the stars are all just different parts of the same stuff, always changing. The energy in the sun today might be in a person tomorrow and in an animal the day after. It's all one big mass of matter, just called different names and forms. These names aren't real because everything is always changing. From another perspective, the universe is like a sea of thoughts, and each of us is a point called a mind. When we see things clearly and free ourselves from illusions, the universe becomes pure and unchanging, immortal. So, what about the idea that when we die, we go to heaven or some other place? It doesn't fit with this understanding.

The concept that we become ghosts or animals after death doesn't hold up. How can something infinite like us come and go? It's like asking why the earth doesn't fall; a meaningless question because there's no "up" or "down" in the universe. Similarly, asking about birth and death for the soul is nonsensical. The soul is everywhere, so where could it go? All this talk of heaven, higher worlds, and lower realms is just a childish illusion. It disappears when we understand our true nature.

The idea that we are just bodies is a big lie. We are the God of the universe. Worshipping God is worshipping our hidden self. Thinking we're born sinners is also a lie. Only those who see sin in others are the real sinners. The universe is seen differently by different people; the wicked see it as hell, the partially good see it as heaven, but the perfect beings see it as God Himself.

When we realize our true nature, we understand we are everywhere, beyond time and space, higher than heaven, and more infinite than anything. Then, fear and suffering end forever. Birth and death, pleasure and pain, earth and heaven – they all vanish. The universe disappears, and so do our identities as men, gods, or demons. We become fearless and free. All illusions and miseries disappear.

Just as clouds pass in the sky, visions of earth, heavens, gods, pleasures, and pains come before the soul and then fade away, leaving the unchanging sky. It's wrong to think we're impure or limited. The real essence of a person is the one Unit Existence.

Can we realize this truth? Yes. Some people already have. Do they die right after? Not right away. It's like stopping one wheel of a moving cart – the other keeps going for a while due to its momentum. Similarly, realizing our true nature keeps the body and mind going until their past actions run out of momentum. Then, freedom is attained while still alive. It's like finding unexpected beauty during a desert journey.

One day, the illusion of this world will break, but it will come back again because our bodies are under the influence of past actions. As long as we're tied to our past actions, everything – people, animals, plants, our attachments, and responsibilities will keep coming back to us, but not as strongly. With a new understanding, the power of past actions weakens. Now we see the difference between reality and illusion more clearly.

Understanding that the soul is beyond laws can lead some to think they can do anything. But while the soul is naturally free, this doesn't mean we're free from responsibility. Even though we feel free in daily life, we're still constrained by laws and circumstances. The essence of a person is always free, but in the world of illusion, we become bound by laws. Our will may be limited, but our true nature is eternally free. Even in our earthly existence, we feel this inner freedom and strive towards it. Once someone attains their true freedom, no law can bind them because they realize the universe itself is theirs.

Evil and good are both parts of the soul, but evil is like an outer layer, while good is closer to the real essence of a person, the Self. To reach the Self, one must first overcome evil, and then embrace goodness. Only after passing through both can a person truly understand themselves. When someone reaches the Self, what remains attached to them? Just a little bit of past actions, but it's all good. Until all bad influences are gone, it's hard to see and understand the truth. So, someone who has found the truth still carries the good parts of their past actions, even if they continue to live and work in this world.

He is everything, so how can he have small ideas about sex or nationality? Stating "I am a man," "I am a woman," or "I am from this country" are all assertions devoid of truth. The soul has no gender and is eternally pure. It's a lie to identify with any gender or nationality because the whole world is our country, and the entire universe is ours. When a person sees God in themselves and others, love grows stronger. The wife loves her husband more when she sees him as God. Similarly, the husband loves his wife more when he sees her as God. This love extends to children, enemies, and everyone else, as they are all seen as manifestations of the divine.

This realization changes everything. Pain and misery vanish, and the struggles of life become like a game. The world becomes beautiful, and peace reigns instead of fighting and quarrelling. With divine realization, hate, jealousy, and evil disappear, and love becomes the guiding force for humanity. If even a small fraction of people in the world recognizes the divinity within themselves and others, the world will change rapidly. Instead of hatred and jealousy, people will see everything as manifestations of the divine. Goodness shall triumph, and evil shall fade away.

These truths, though ancient, are universal. They will spread throughout the world, becoming accessible to everyone regardless of their background. They will transform society and uplift humanity, bringing unity and love to all. Only the person who sees the One in this world of many, who recognizes the Living Being among the lifeless, and who grasps Reality amid the shadows, will find eternal peace - no one else.

First, people believed in a personal God outside the universe. Then, they realized God was within the universe. Finally, they understood that the soul itself is one with God, connecting all the different parts of the universe. The person who sees a single thread running through the diversity of the world, who finds infinite life amidst death, and who discovers light and knowledge in a world of darkness and ignorance, will attain eternal peace. This peace belongs to no one else but them.

INTENTION

"Intentions define our essence; they unveil our truest form. What we think about ourselves, we intend accordingly."

My main idea is acceptance, not exclusion.

I don't just believe in tolerating others because that can be disrespectful. I believe in accepting them as they are.

Why should I just tolerate someone?

It's like saying I think they're wrong, but I'll let them live anyway.

I accept all religions from the past and worship alongside them.

I worship God in whatever form people worship Him.

I'll visit a mosque, a church, or a Buddhist temple and pray with them.

I'll even meditate in the forest.

And I'll keep my heart open to whatever new spiritual revelations may come in the future.

God's book isn't finished; it's an ongoing revelation.

I am the universe in its current state, in constant flux.

Beyond change and attributes, eternally flawless, eternally blessed.

I am everywhere at all times, existing eternally.
There's nowhere I haven't already reached.

The human self, or soul, is supreme, surpassing all gods, past, present, and future.

Its magnificence exceeds even the vast universe.

I bow to no one but myself, if I bow other that is also to myself.

I recognise the divine within.

I find strength and guidance from the Infinite Being inside me and others.

I am the one eating through millions of mouths, so how can I be hungry?

I work through countless hands, so how can I be inactive?

I live the life of the entire universe, so where is death for me?

I am beyond life and death.

I am naturally free; nothing can bind me, not even the God of this universe.

The scriptures are like small maps trying to describe my greatness, but I am the only existence in the universe.

So, what use are these books to me?

I am Existence Absolute, Bliss Absolute, Knowledge Absolute.

I am He. Like a lion breaking its cage, I break my chains and am free forever. Nothing frightens me, nothing holds me down.

Only ignorance and delusion have no power over me.

I am the Pure One, the Ever-blessed.

I am free, and my freedom is constant—it has been and always will be.

I am in charge of my destiny;

I create my own good and bad.

I am pure and blessed.

I am beyond death and fear, beyond labels like caste or creed.

I am not bound by virtue or vice, happiness or misery.

Rituals and traditions don't control me.

I don't experience hunger or thirst; my identity isn't bound to my body.

I am pure bliss.

I have discovered a sense of unity and oneness throughout the universe in what is known as the Impersonal Absolute.

I choose to believe that my freedom is real, and any sense of bondage is an illusion.

My body is my temple
The world around me, my sacred space.
My words weave magic,
Every thought a seed of intention.
My deeds are sacred rituals,
Bringing forth what is meant to be.
I am divine, I am sacred.

I'm here to experience life,
To laugh, to learn,
To love, and to celebrate.
To grow and expand,
For I hold power within.
In this realization,
I am liberated.

I willingly let go of what no longer serves me, making room for what truly inspires me.

I embrace myself and my beliefs.

It's my concern and duty for me to embrace me.

I feel because I came here to heal.

My gift is sensitivity, allowing me to comprehend others deeply.

I embody love.

My energy reveals what I need to know to contribute to healing the world.

I have moments of darkness and negativity, but I also embody qualities of kindness, generosity, and peace.

I believe in embracing all aspects of myself, acknowledging that both light and shadow coexist within me.

Life's journey involves finding equilibrium between these contrasting elements, recognizing that each contributes to the richness of human experience.

I allow others to be themselves.

I allow myself to be me.

I don't rush things.

Solutions will show up.

It's okay not to know everything -

I accept it.

I don't push things anymore.

Whatever happens, happens.

I only make room for what's meant for me, with energy and space.

I am strong, not just born, but made.
Every challenge I face builds my mind and heart.
I stride ahead, proud and powerful.
I've weathered storms and emerged a warrior!

I'm the source of my own power.

I've been searching for meaning, exploring universities and seeking guidance from others.

Yet, I found true wisdom when I listened to my soul's whispers in silence.

I understand this change is hard, but if I'm not breaking apart;

I'm evolving into something new, with a fresh ability to shine beautifully.

I questioned why I was given just "this." A voice responded, "Only 'this' will guide you to 'that'."

No matter how much you study me, you won't truly know me, as I am different in countless ways from what you perceive. Try seeing through my eyes to understand me, for I inhabit a realm beyond your sight.

After facing tough times and coming out stronger, I now walk with the boldness of a leader, the courage of a hero, and the strength of a warrior.

I understand that not everyone may be ready for my voice, as it pierces through illusions and uncovers raw truths. Similarly, not everyone may be prepared for my energy, which radiates innocence, untainted by society's weight and generational wounds, creating space for transformation. Despite this, it's a delight when someone embraces all of this and meets me where I am.

I'm not healing just to deal with tough times.

I'm used to those.

I'm healing to handle and enjoy the good times that come my way.

I've faced countless challenges and emerged anew each time, striving to improve upon my past self. From breakdowns,

I've found the strength to rebuild and redefine myself. Amidst the shadows,

I've discovered my own inner light.

The Universe entrusts me with wealth to make a meaningful difference in the world.

I embrace the journey of discovering my passion, which is not just about careers and money, but about reconnecting with my authentic self, buried beneath the needs of others.

I am here to prioritize understanding myself, rather than seeking to be understood by others.

Bitterness reveals where I need healing and where I still hold judgments, towards others and myself. Resentment highlights when I dwell on the past, neglecting the present. Discomfort signals the need to pay attention to the present moment, offering a chance to change my approach. Anger illuminates my passions, boundaries, and beliefs for change. Disappointment signifies my efforts and refusal to succumb to apathy. Guilt indicates living by others' expectations, not my own. Shame reminds me to reconnect with my true self, free from others' perceptions. Anxiety prompts me to wake up, be present, and overcome fear.

Sadness showcases the depth of my emotions and care for others and the world.

I am the all-seeing Seer, witnessing the entirety of existence.

I am the Source, creating all beings and worlds.

I encompass the states of waking, dreaming, and deep sleep.

I exist across all dimensions, infinite and profound.

I transcend the manifested world, existing in the unmanifest.

I am the Infinity of Creation, uniting all in oneness.

I am both beyond and within, eternal and limitless.

I am the essence of time, both its roar and its silence.

I am the manifestation of everything, yet I am nothing.

I am the Knower of all knowledge, the seed within all creation.

I am the background of existence, the eternal essence

I am the dancer of the cosmic play, the night and the day.

I encompass illusions and the essence of all.

I am the unseen Seer, witnessing all that ever was.

I am the mysterious source of Universe, the eternal I am.

I release self-imposed chains and step into the light of freedom.

I am liberated from negative thoughts, doubt, worry, and anxiety.

I am newly born into the spirit of freedom.

I declare my independence and celebrate the good in my life.

I release fear and proclaim my independence.

I remove barriers to love, joy, peace, harmony, and vibrant health.

I turn to the Divine within, recognizing freedom as my natural state.

I am not the body; I am beyond physical form.

I am not the emotion, nor the passing thoughts; I transcend the fluctuations of the mind.

The mind is merely a subtle instrument of the soul; I am the essence of the soul itself.

I embody spiritual essence, infused with divine intelligence, love, and power.

I am unified with my Higher Soul, resonating with the eternal essence of existence.

I affirm: "I AM THE UNIVERSE," embodying the divine spark within me.

I am connected with God, one with the divine presence within and around me.

I am one with all, experiencing the interconnectedness of all existence.

I am awake, fully aware of my role as the creator of universes. I embrace my consciousness and command my abilities for the betterment of all, both in this life and beyond. I embody the pure essence of love, creating, giving, and receiving love abundantly. I am a survivor, a believer, a warrior with a clear path, and nothing will obstruct my journey to my higher self.

Love is my eternal mantra, my constant hymn, resonating within and echoing throughout the universe. My heartbeat aligns with the rhythm of the cosmos, as the universe mirrors the depths of my soul. I affirm that my body is the true embodiment of my soul, and this alignment is my greatest manifestation.

Breathing in, I acknowledge that peace is present within me.

Breathing out, I recognize that peace is my essence, not any fleeting emotion.

Breathing in, I am aware that tranquillity brings comfort.

Breathing out, I trust that serenity will prevail as emotions shift.

Breathing in, I embrace calmness as my natural state.

I am eternal, existing beyond the boundaries of time.

I am divine, connected to the sacred essence of the universe.

I am transcendent, rising above earthly limitations.

I am free, liberated from all constraints that hold me back.

I am love, radiating boundless compassion and warmth to all beings.

I am magical, embracing the wonder and enchantment of life.

I am creative, channelling my unique ideas and talents to create beauty and joy.

I am powerful, capable of achieving my dreams and shaping my reality.

I embody eternal peace, cultivating inner serenity and radiating peace to all beings.

I see divine essence in all beings, cultivating love and compassion transcending outer appearances.

I release the illusion of birth and death, living fearlessly knowing my true essence is timeless.

I acknowledge the illusion of separateness, cultivating empathy and compassion as expressions of divine unity.

I honour each individual's unique journey towards self-realization, offering guidance with compassion and trust in their wisdom.

I celebrate diversity, encouraging harmony and mutual respect among all beliefs and perspectives.

My actions sculpt my character, guiding my soul's evolution towards freedom and self-realization

As I release the illusion of separateness, my true Self shines forth with brilliance, tapping into infinite wisdom and love for self-realization.

Selflessness guides me to embrace collective well-being, transcending ego. I align with the unity of all existence by relinquishing the notion of a separate self.

I acknowledge the interconnectedness of all beings, fuelling my commitment to acts of kindness and compassion. In serving others,

I serve the universal consciousness that binds us.

NIRVANA SHATAKAM

(Translated Version)

I am not the mind, the intellect, the ego, or the memory;

I am not the senses or the elements of earth, water, fire, air, or ether.

I am pure consciousness, bliss, and eternal freedom.

I am Shiva, I am Shiva.

I am not the breath nor the five vital airs;

I am not the seven elements, nor the five sheaths of the body.

I am not the speech, nor the hands, nor the feet, nor the anus, nor the genitals.

I am pure consciousness, bliss, and eternal freedom.

I am Shiva, I am Shiva.

There is no form or shape to me, no cause or effect, no karma or liberation; I have no father, mother, relatives, or friend.

I am pure consciousness, bliss, and eternal freedom.

I am Shiva, I am Shiva.

I am beyond the cycle of birth and death, beyond all sense of duality, beyond all fear, beyond all attachment;

I am beyond the mind, beyond the intellect, beyond the ego, beyond the body.

I am pure consciousness, bliss, and eternal freedom.

I am Shiva, I am Shiva.

I am neither bound nor free, neither seeking liberation nor enjoying worldly pleasures;

I am neither righteous nor unrighteous, neither virtuous nor sinful.

I am pure consciousness, bliss, and eternal freedom.

I am Shiva, I am Shiva.

I am neither the doer nor the enjoyer, neither the enjoyer of the fruits of actions nor the one who suffers from their consequences;

I am neither the doer of good deeds nor the doer of bad deeds.

I am pure consciousness, bliss, and eternal freedom.

I am Shiva, I am Shiva.